Making Spirits

Piano Solos for Christmas

Arranged by Marilynn Ham

CONTENTS

A CHRISTMAS PROCESSIONAL 2
  O Come, All Ye Faithful/Joyful, Joyful, We Adore Thee

STAR MEDLEY 7
  Twinkle, Twinkle, Little Star/The Star Carol/Do You Hear What I Hear?

JINGLE BELLS 12

JESUS, JESUS, REST YOUR HEAD 16
  In the setting of Pachelbel's "Canon in D"

THE CHRISTMAS DRUMMER 20
  Pat-a-pan/The Little Drummer Boy

THE ANGELS' GLORIA 24
  Vivaldi's "Gloria"/Angels We Have Heard on High

A CHILD'S CHRISTMAS 30
  Up on the Housetop/Rudolph, the Red-nosed Reindeer/Santa Claus Is Coming to Town

SWEET, HOLY CHILD 36
  Sweet Little Jesus Boy/Infant Holy, Infant Lowly

Copyright © 1995 Lillenas Publishing Co.
All rights reserved. Litho in U.S.A.

KANSAS CITY, MO 64141

*"O Come, All Ye Faithful" (John F. Wade)

*Arr. © 1995 by Lillenas Publishing Co. All rights reserved.
Administered by The Copyright Company, 40 Music Square East, Nashville, TN 37203.

3

*"Joyful, Joyful, We Adore Thee" (Beethoven)

*Arr. © 1995 by Lillenas Publishing Co. All rights reserved.
   Administered by The Copyright Company, 40 Music Square East, Nashville, TN 37203.

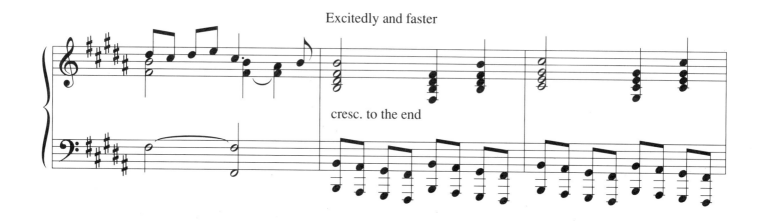

Excitedly and faster

cresc. to the end

For Ellen, Calvin and Grace

Star Medley

Twinkle, Twinkle, Little Star
The Star Carol
Do You Hear What I Hear?

Arr. by Marilynn Ham

*"Twinkle, Twinkle, Little Star" (Traditional)

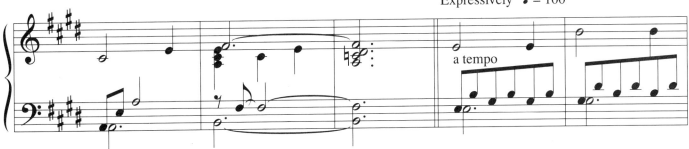

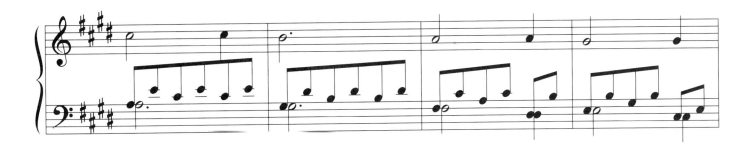

*Arr. © 1995 by Lillenas Publishing Co. All rights reserved.
Administered by The Copyright Company, 40 Music Square East, Nashville, TN 37203.

*"The Star Carol" (Alfred Burt)

*© 1954 (renewed) and 1957 (renewed) Hollis Music, Inc., New York, NY. International copyright secured.
All rights reserved, including public performance for profit. Reprinted by permission.

*"Do You Hear What I Hear?" (Gloria Shayne and Noel Regney)

*© 1962 Regent Music Corp. Copyright renewed by Jewel Music Publishing Co., Inc.
All rights reserved. Used by permission.

For Sarah, Catherine and George
Jingle Bells

J. PIERPONT
Arr. by Marilynn Ham

14

For Gregory

Jesus, Jesus, Rest Your Head
(In the setting of Pachelbel's *Canon in D*)

Appalachian Carol
Arr. by Marilynn Ham

Arr. © 1995 by Lillenas Publishing Co. All rights reserved.
Administered by The Copyright Company, 40 Music Square East, Nashville, TN 37203.

For Kristine and Jacob

The Christmas Drummer
Pat-a-pan
The Little Drummer Boy

Arr. by Marilynn Ham

*"Pat-a-pan" (Traditional)

*Arr. © 1995 by Lillenas Publishing Co. All rights reserved.
Administered by The Copyright Company, 40 Music Square East, Nashville, TN 37203.

22

*"The Little Drummer Boy" (Katherine K. Davis, Harry Simeone and Henry Onorati)

* Copyright 1958, 1960 by Mills Music, Inc. and International Korwin Corp.
    International copyright secured. Made in the USA. All rights reserved. Used by permission.

For Norris and Meryl

The Angels' Gloria

Vivaldi's "Gloria"
Angels We Have Heard on High

Arr. by Marilynn Ham

Allegro ♩ = 112

*"Gloria" (Vivaldi)

f Play all 8th notes detached

*Arr. © 1995 by Lillenas Publishing Co. All rights reserved.
Administered by The Copyright Company, 40 Music Square East, Nashville, TN 37203.

*"Angels We Have Heard on High" (Trad. French Melody)

*Arr. © 1995 by Lillenas Publishing Co. All rights reserved.
Administered by The Copyright Company, 40 Music Square East, Nashville, TN 37203.

For Keith, Heather, Kevin and Holly

A Child's Christmas

Up on the Housetop
Rudolph, The Red-nosed Reindeer
Santa Claus Is Coming to Town

Arr. by Marilynn Ham

*"Up on the Housetop" (Benjamin Russell Hanby)

*Arr. © 1995 by Lillenas Publishing Co. All rights reserved.
Administered by The Copyright Company, 40 Music Square East, Nashville, TN 37203.

*"Rudolph, the Red-nosed Reindeer" (Johnny Marks)

*Copyright © 1949, renewed 1977 St. Nicholas Music, Inc., 1619 Broadway, New York, NY 10019. All rights reserved. Used by permission.

*"Santa Claus Is Coming to Town" (J. Fred Coots and Haven Gillespie)

*© 1934 (renewed 1962) Leo Feist, Inc. Rights of Leo Feist, Inc. assigned to EMI Catalog Partnership and controlled and administered by EMI Feist Catalog, Inc. Rights for the extended renewal term in the US controlled by Haven Gillespie Music and EMI Feist Catalog, Inc. This arrangement © 1991 and 1995 Haven Gillespie Music and EMI Feist Catalog, Inc. All rights reserved. Used by permission.

*"Santa Claus Is Coming to Town" (J. Fred Coots and Haven Gillespie)

*© 1934 (renewed 1962) Leo Feist, Inc. Rights of Leo Feist, Inc. assigned to EMI Catalog Partnership and controlled and administered by EMI Feist Catalog, Inc. Rights for the extended renewal term in the US controlled by Haven Gillespie Music and EMI Feist Catalog, Inc. This arrangement © 1991 and 1995 Haven Gillespie Music and EMI Feist Catalog, Inc. All rights reserved. Used by permission.

*"Infant Holy, Infant Lowly" (Polish Carol)

*Arr. © 1995 by Lillenas Publishing Co. All rights reserved.
   Administered by The Copyright Company, 40 Music Square East, Nashville, TN 37202.